THE BEE BOOK

A Tale of Leadership and Change

By Craig Smith and Paul Rigby

www.thebeebook.com

Illustrated by Vincent Moses Raja
Book design by Sel P

ISBN: 978-1519529183

For additional information:

Visit *www.thebeebook.com* to find out more about The Bee Book and how you can use it to drive change in your organisation.

Email us at *info@thebeebook.com*

THE BEE BOOK OVERVIEW

A hive of bees is faced with a catastrophic change in their environment. The bees need to take quick action if they are to survive. But is the hive ready and capable of adapting to the challenges presented or are they stuck in a world of complacency?

The Bee Book takes an unconventional look at the challenges organisations face when trying to adapt to a rapidly changing and unpredictable world. This short story will challenge your thinking and ask questions of how you deal with change, innovation, leadership and employee engagement in your organisation.

WHAT PEOPLE ARE SAYING ABOUT THE BEE BOOK:

The concepts and suggestions are simple, yet powerful, and it's because they are simple that they are appealing. The Bee Book gave me a renewed energy personally and professionally at a time I needed it most. If each of our leaders chooses to act as they should instead of deferring on decisions and stifling innovation, we will see very positive outcomes for our company!

– Human Resources Director

....

This was a great opportunity to really understand that we must first engage people if we want them to change.

– Learning and Performance Manager

....

The Bee Book re-energised my passion at work. It brought home a few truths and challenges that I had been ignoring. It was beyond my expectations. Thank you for bringing my passion back to my work.

– Senior Project Manager

....

V

The Bee Book makes you look at the way things are being done and then how things can be different and better.

– Vice President of Operations

....

ACKNOWLEDGEMENTS

We would like to thank a number of people who have helped us to get this book written and published.

We'd like to thank Kay and Helen who have been our proof readers, bee image approvers and supporters. We value your input and guidance.

Special thanks to our editor Thomas who was patient, creative and firm when we strayed off the straight and narrow. We wish to pay special credit to Vincent Moses Raja for producing the wonderful images for the book. His ability to visualise the characters in the story left us in awe. Big thanks also to Pandiselvi for his excellent formatting and design of the book layout itself.

Final thanks go to our friends and clients who gave us the initial feedback on our ideas and sparked new thoughts and storylines. We'd like to mention Kristien, Julie, Caroline, Antoinette, Tijen and Özkan for their help and advice.

FOREWORD

We wrote this allegory (some will refer to it as a fable or parable) to help people in all types of organisations: whether it is a large multi-national, a not-for-profit, a school, a government department or a start-up. We feel that understanding the basic ingredients for taking an organisation from where it is today to where it should be tomorrow is a critical leadership role.

We have found that allegories allow readers to learn more effectively by losing themselves in the story and being able to relate to the characters. It also helps them to understand how core principles may be applied in real-world scenarios. It quickens the learning process and makes it fun and interesting at the same time. Furthermore, it makes the whole experience memorable.

So, here you have a quick and easy-to-read story about change and leadership. The Bee Book covers the typical issues that occur every day in our working lives.

The story is about a hive of bees who are faced with a catastrophic change in their environment. They need to take quick action if they are to survive. But is the hive ready and capable of adapting to the challenges presented or are they stuck in a world of complacency?

The main characters – Buzz, Stripes, Hover, Greybee, Queen Luna, Queen Sola, Mr. Wingit, Zippy and a few others – represent typical employees in any organisation, people you may know. Perhaps you can even identify yourself in the story.

The challenges they face vary from general leadership issues, decision-making, complacency, innovation, change, employee engagement and just making simple common sense decisions that any organisation needs to make on a daily basis. We encounter procrastinators, positive outliers, fence-sitters and a hierarchical decision-making process. All play an important part in whether or not the hive will survive.

The Bee Book may be enjoyed by anyone. It does not contain a prescriptive set of lessons that one can copy from a page at the back of the book. It has been written for you to interpret and translate with your colleagues and workmates if you believe its lessons will benefit your organisation. The lessons will become evident as you progress through the book. Each person will have his or her own perspective on how best to handle the challenges and will identify different potential solutions. After all, in today's complex world, there is no one right or wrong way to accomplish the end result and not every challenge is obvious to everyone. We are all individuals striving to do the best we can.

To complement The Bee Book, we have developed an interactive workshop for leaders which facilitates discussions about similarities in the book to your organisational issues. The workshop brings The Bee Book and characters to life. We use examples from the story to challenge the organisational habits you face in the real world. Through effective dialogue, we help you to arrive at solutions that will take you on the next phase of your journey - wherever that may be.

At our website (*www.thebeebook.com*) you will find lots of useful resources to use alongside The Bee Book to drive change in your organisation. You can find more information about this at the end of the book on page 109.

If you have any questions about the book, the website or "The Bee Book" training programme, please visit *www.thebeebook.com* or email *info@thebeebook.com*.

So sit back and enjoy our tale. You will have fun along the way. Fun is good – right? We certainly had fun writing this book.

THE BEE BOOK GLOSSARY
(AND SOME OF THE CHARACTERS)

Farmer John   An external power that can dramatically influence and change something we depend on for future success.

KPIs   Key performance indicators. A measure of individual targets.

Luna Hive   A traditional, hierarchical, workplace where success has always been assured and the market always stable... but where complacency is possible.

Sola Hive   A workplace where employees are engaged, motivated and have the authority to make decisions. An environment that has changed many times and where employees have learnt to adapt.

MBeeA A Master of Business Administration in bee world. Seen as an indication of executive competence.

Nectar A sugar-rich liquid produced by plants in glands called nectaries. Nectar is the sugar source for honey. A precious resource, essential for survival.

Appraisal system A methodology used to measure performance.

Smith's field Represents new opportunities, challenges and new markets… and also risk.

Paradigm paralysis The inability or refusal to see beyond the present situation.

Scouts Employees who look for new opportunities – they are focused on tomorrow, the future. They are positive outliers.

Collectors Employees who focus on today's activities to keep the business running today. Typically called the 'performance engine'. Their mantra is on time, on spec and on budget.

Slackers   People who are active but not
                    productive.

Polly   Just another concerned employee
                    … er … bee at the Luna hive.

Zag   Supply chain manager at the Luna
                    hive. He does enough not to get
                    fired.

Digger and   Typical workers in the Luna hive
Mason   with the potential to offer more
                    than they are asked or expected to
                    do.

TABLE OF CONTENTS

INTRODUCING THE MAIN CAST IN ORDER OF APPEARANCE

Buzz

Our hero. Front line worker in the Luna hive. Someone who cares about his hive and believes in making things better. A positive outlier in a traditional organisation.

Stripes

Front line worker in the Luna hive. Dedicated,
hardworking and loyal.

Queen Luna

Leader of the Luna hive. Traditional, cares for her hive but insulated from realities.

Hover

Middle Manager in the Luna hive. Hardworking but traditional. Reluctant to take risks.

Greybee

Senior Manager at the Luna hive. Risk-averse.
Doesn't like to give bad news and wants to insulate
Queen Luna from external issues.

Mr Wingit

Consultant who "wings-it" or as they say "makes it up as he goes along". Has made a living from telling clients what they want to hear or presenting stock answers to complex problems.

Leadbottom

A Luna hive manager from the old school who struggles with change. Committed but lacks the support or skills to adapt to new ways of working.

Zippy

A typical worker bee from the Sola hive who is used to new ways of working. He has autonomy to make things happen and is happy and engaged in what he does.

Queen Sola

Leader of the Sola hive. A forward thinking
leader who engages her team and inspires them
to take action.

CHAPTER 1

"BARREN SOIL"

With a sinking feeling, Buzz surveyed the scene before him.

The reports had been true. In fact, it was even worse than he expected.

What had once been a vast meadow of blooming flowers, each bursting with precious nectar, was now a wasteland of barren soil. As far as the eye could see there was nothing but the straight rows of earth scarred by the iron plough of Farmer John.

Not a single blossom remained.

"How could he do this?" said Buzz to Stripes.

Stripes shrugged. "It's been said that Farmer John wants to use this field to plant corn. But the reasons don't matter. All that matters is that we've got a disaster on our hands. We'd better get back to the hive and give them the bad news."

In silence they turned and took flight.

For as long as Buzz could remember, Farmer John's wildflower meadow had provided Queen Luna's hive with a steady supply of the high-quality nectar the hive needed to produce its grade-A honey. The flowers bloomed from Spring until Autumn and bees from the Luna hive and other hives from around the area went there to collect the nectar and use it to produce honey. It was a system that had worked smoothly season after season, producing enough wealth for every hive.

Now the system was broken. To Buzz and Stripes, the future seemed bleak.

As they made the short flight back to the hive, the two bees hoped that Queen Luna would provide an answer. After all, she was the leader and had final authority on all matters pertaining to the hive. Organisation, production, sales - all were under her direct command. While she had her advisors, ultimately she made the final decisions.

Soon the neat white box of the hive came into view. The moment Buzz and Stripes landed, other bees crowded around them.

"What did you see?" asked one.

"Is it as bad as they say?" asked another.

"Are we going out of business?" demanded a third.

"All right, all right, go back to your posts," said Hover as he approached the crowd. "Let's not get excited. Everything will be fine. Just return to work, all of you. Buzz and Stripes, please come with me."

As the crowd dispersed, Hover said to the two bees, "I'm taking you to see Greybee. She's a senior advisor to the Queen. You can give her your report."

Buzz and Stripes nervously followed Hover. Since he was their division leader, they knew him well, but they had never met Greybee. The top bees - Queen Luna and her staff - worked in a separate executive wing of the hive and ordinary bees like Buzz and Stripes only saw them at a distance during special events, like the annual Hive party.

"How do I look?" whispered Buzz to Stripes. "Do I have any pollen stuck to my legs?"

"No, you're good," replied Stripes. "How are my antennae?"

"They look fine," smiled Buzz.

After making their way along busy corridors - with Hover telling the bees they saw along the way not to worry and to return to their stations - they came to an ornate door. Using his swipe card, Hover opened the door and invited Buzz and Stripes to enter.

With wings carefully folded they entered the executive suite.

"It certainly is grand in here," whispered Stripes.

They stopped at a reception desk. "Greybee is expecting us," said Hover to the receptionist.

"Yes, you can go right in," came the reply.

"What are we going to say to Greybee?" whispered Buzz to Stripes as they walked down a long corridor. "No one ever gives the bosses bad news. She's going to sting us!"

"We'll just have to do the best we can," replied Stripes.

After passing through another expensive-looking door they entered a big office. The air was cool and the walls were decorated with beautifully framed images of flowers, with each one carefully labelled by species. In a glass case were displayed an assortment of the very finest jars of Luna branded honey.

Behind a desk sat a bee who, judging by her expensive coat and gleaming wings, was wealthy and successful. The framed certificate for her MBeeA hung prominently on the wall.

"Ah, Hover, thank you for coming," said Greybee as she clicked her computer mouse.

"I've brought Buzz and Stripes," said Hover. "They have just returned from the wildflower meadow."

"What did you see there?" asked Greybee.

Buzz nervously stepped forward. "Well, umm, the field - well, the field has changed."

"What do you mean, 'the field has changed'?" said Greybee.

Buzz shot a glance at Stripes. She was looking at the floor.

Buzz looked at Hover. He was looking at some notes.

"Well, it's not exactly the same as it used to be," stammered Buzz.

Greybee frowned. She switched her attention to Stripes. "You there - I'm sorry, what is your name again?"

"Stripes."

"Yes, of course. Stripes. Can you tell me what you saw at the wildflower meadow?"

"I'm sure it's nothing," mumbled Stripes. "It's just that - well, all the flowers are gone."

Greybee stood up. She turned to Hover. "What does this bee mean when she says, 'All the flowers are gone'? It's the middle of summer - the height of the season. We have quotas to meet. It's inconceivable that the flowers are gone."

Hover cleared his throat. "It's true. The flowers are gone. Farmer John has ploughed them into the ground. The field is barren. Not a single living plant remains."

Greybee stood and glared at them. One of her pearlescent wings twitched. There was an awkward pause while she pondered the situation.

"Okay," she said evenly. "Here's what we're going to do. I'm going to take this information to the Queen's council. The council will formulate an appropriate response. Meanwhile, I ask you three to go about your normal duties and say *nothing* about this. We do not want to cause unrest in the hive. This information is on a need-to-know basis. Understand? At the appropriate time, the council spokesperson will inform the hive of the situation and the steps we intend to take. It will be an orderly and business-like process. Meanwhile, we need to maintain production. Hover, what's our nectar reserve?"

"I'm not sure," replied Hover.

"You're not sure?" asked Greybee. "Don't we know how much nectar we have in reserve?"

Hover shuffled through his papers. "The most recent report I have is from the previous quarter," he replied. "It indicates that we have a one-month supply. But there may have been spoilage and one of the tanks has a leak. So we're not sure."

"Well, take a guess," said Greybee.

"I'd guess three weeks," replied Hover.

"Okay, three weeks," said Greybee. She entered the figure into her spreadsheet. "We have to make some adjustments in our 'KPIs'," she muttered to no one in particular.

Buzz and Stripes looked blankly at each other.

"KPIs... you know... key performance indicators, targets, measures of success... for goodness sakes" added Greybee, clearly frustrated at the two workers' inability to understand her use of acronyms. "If we're facing reduced production, we'll need to raise our prices and cut back expenses. This will include a reduction in labour costs, of course."

"Yes, of course," said Hover. He swallowed hard. He knew what that meant: layoffs and slashed salaries.

"The Queen's tenth anniversary celebration is scheduled for the end of the summer," said Greybee. "We need it to be a joyous occasion. We've got special guests and important bees coming from all over the region. We really need to focus on protecting this historic milestone. If we cannot meet our KPIs, we'll have to make the necessary cuts. It's just a fact of life."

"Yes," agreed Hover. "A fact of life."

"Very well," said Greybee. "That will be all. You may go now. And don't forget - this information is confidential."

"I understand," replied Hover. "Confidential."

After they had made their way out of the executive suite and back to the employees' area of the hive, Buzz turned to Hover.

"Confidential?" he asked incredulously. "Is she kidding?"

Hover looked around them. "Sssh," he said. "We're in a public place. I understand how you feel, but I'm sure that Greybee knows what she's doing. She's an experienced administrator. Let's just keep cool and do what we're told."

"But we've got bees flying to the wildflower meadow every day!" said Stripes. "How is this supposed to be kept a secret? The disaster is right out there for everyone to see!"

"We've changed flight assignments," replied Hover. "We've also told everyone that Farmer John used some insecticide on the meadow and it's temporarily closed. No one will go near there, believe me. It will give the hive leadership time to figure out what to do."

Buzz looked at Stripes. There was nothing they could do.

CHAPTER 2

"THE 'WINGIT' PLAN"

The next morning, Hover, Buzz and Stripes were again summoned to the office of Greybee. They joined a group of executive bees, most of whom Buzz and Stripes had never met before.

"Thank you for coming," said Greybee from behind her big desk. She eyed Buzz and Stripes. "As I'm sure you know," she said to them, "normally these executive sessions are attended only by upper management. But in this case, since you're familiar with the situation, we thought it prudent to allow you to represent the employees."

"Thank you," said Stripes.

"Now then," said Greybee, "in response to the dramatic and unfortunate change in external conditions - specifically, the reduction in our supply of locally sourced nectar - the Queen directed me to engage the services of an esteemed management consultant. He comes very highly recommended and I'm sure we're all interested in his report. Allow me to introduce Mr. Wingit."

A bee wearing a set of expensive wings stepped forward.

"Look at his antennae," whispered Buzz to Stripes. "I'll bet you anything they're fake."

"Quiet," replied Stripes. "You'll get us thrown out of here!"

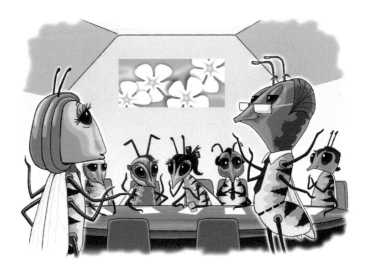

Wingit cleared his throat. "Thank you, Greybee. As a professional productivity expert, I've been asked to analyse the threat posed by the closure of Farmer John's wildflower meadow and make my recommendations. To that end, having cross-referenced the matrix of inputs as they leverage the cost of lost opportunities across the spectrum of production capacity, I've developed a set of key performance indicators that exhibit a better-than-random qualitative potential to increase both earned and residual revenues."

"Is that clear to everyone?" asked Greybee.

All of the executives nodded their heads.

"It wasn't clear to *me*," whispered Buzz to Stripes. "Was he speaking English?"

"We're front-line bees," replied Stripes. "Maybe we're not supposed to understand this technical business stuff."

"More specifically," said Wingit, "my goal has been to identify efficiency savings for the hive, instigate a workflow reorganisation and increase productivity. To that end, I have made a set of recommendations. You have them on the printed handout."

The executive bees looked at each other. There was no handout.

Greybee grabbed a stack of papers from her desk. "Here they are. Sorry about that. Hover, will you please make sure everyone has a copy? Wingit, please continue."

"Thank you," said Wingit. "I have made a set of six recommendations. They are as follows:

 A downsizing and a larvae freeze to reduce bee numbers. This will cut expenses.

2 A strict 'need to know' communication policy within the hive in order to reduce uncertainty and control anxiety. We cannot allow rampant rumours to disrupt the hive and, even worse, leak out and negatively affect our marketplace and our investors.

3 A reorganisation of the hive to set up new functions and management structure.

4 An enhanced employee appraisal system and bonus scheme. This will both increase bee engagement and reduce turnover during this challenging period.

5 A new information technology system to better control productivity.

6 A new set of key performance indicators that will allow Luna hive to maintain a positive posture in the investment community and maintain the integrity of the Luna brand in the marketplace."

The assembled executive bees nodded and talked quietly amongst themselves as they digested this new set of proposals.

"I don't get it," whispered Buzz to Stripes. "What does any of this have to do with Farmer John ploughing up his wildflowers? Isn't that the problem?"

"Beats me," replied Stripes. "I suppose they need to do things their own way. But it certainly seems like a waste of time."

Greybee stood up. "Thank you, Wingit, for your report and your recommendations. It looks like a very solid plan. Are there any questions?"

None of the bees responded.

Tentatively, Buzz raised one of his six arms.

Greybee nodded to him. "Buzz, what's your question?"

"It seems to me that the problem facing us is pretty simple: Farmer John ploughed his wildflower meadow into the ground. But there could be other fields. Perhaps further away and more difficult to get to, but they might exist. And of course the variety of flowers in these other fields might be slightly different from those that were in Farmer John's, which could affect the taste of our product. But I'm sure that if..."

Greybee waved her antennae. "Yes, yes, thank you, Buzz. I thought you had a question about the plan. The plan that has been developed at great expense by our professional consultant."

Buzz looked at the assembled executive bees. They were all staring at him. "I'm sorry," he said. "I really don't have a question. The plan sounds good. *Really* good."

Greybee smiled. "Excellent. I knew we'd all agree. That's important, isn't it? That we all agree?"

The executive bees nodded.

"Fine," said Greybee. "I'll inform the Queen that we have adopted the Wingit plan. I'm sure she'll be both very pleased and relieved not to have to worry about this little problem."

With heavy hearts Buzz and Stripes returned to the employees' section of the hive. In the lunchroom their colleagues were gathered around the old-fashioned bulletin board where notices from management were posted.

"Does anyone know what's going on?" asked a bee.

"I heard something about a disaster at Farmer John's wildflower meadow," replied another.

"My boss said that Farmer John sprayed the field with an insecticide," said a third. "That means we can't go there until after it rains."

"Yeah, but what does that have to do with this corporate reorganisation plan?" asked another. "It says here that I now have to report to the head of flight operations as well as to the head of nectar inventory. It's crazy. I've already got too much paperwork to fill out. It seems as though I spend half my days completing reports. I send them up to the managers, but I never know what happens to them. I think they just get shoved into a drawer somewhere."

"Hey, look it's Buzz and Stripes," said a bee. "They know what's going on. Come on, Buzz, tell us. What's it all about?"

Buzz pondered his dilemma for a moment. His natural inclination was to simply tell the truth: that Farmer John had ploughed up all of the flowers and that Luna hive needed to find new sources of nectar. But he had been told by Greybee to keep the disaster confidential and that there was no sense in needlessly alarming other bees in the hive.

A troubled Buzz decided there was no good answer. He looked into the faces of his friends and colleagues and forced a smile. "Uh, I don't know much about it," he said. "There's a problem with the wildflower meadow. They say it's not serious. All the memos you see posted here are part of a plan that management has embraced. It's called "*the Wingit plan*". That's pretty much the whole story."

With that, Buzz quickly excused himself. Stripes followed him.

"I feel terrible," he said to her when they were alone in the office kitchen. "I just lied to my co-workers."

"You couldn't help it," she said. "Greybee made it clear that she wanted no discussion of the wildflower meadow. You had no choice."

CHAPTER 3

"BUZZY DOING NOTHING"

That afternoon, the mood in the hive was tense. Pending the approval by the flight director of new routes to other, more distant flowerbeds, flights from the hive had been temporarily suspended.

In the lunchroom groups of bees were sitting around talking.

"I have no confidence in the flight director," grumbled one. "It will take old Leadbottom a week to figure out new flight plans. He insists on doing it all by himself. He sits in his office with those old-fashioned charts and maps and uses a ruler to measure the distances. Can you believe it?"

"Can't you get software for route planning?" asked another.

"Of course you can," replied the first bee. "But Leadbottom says, 'This is the way we've always done it.' He'll never change."

A bee studied one of the many memos from Wingit. "It says here that we've got three weeks of nectar reserves," said the bee. "Three weeks? Who are they kidding? Has anyone from management ever set foot in the warehouse?

The place is a mess and the tanks are leaking. I'd say we've got two weeks' worth of reserves at most."

"And thanks to the larvae freeze," said another, "we have no trainees in the nursery. This means that a bunch of new tasks have been added to my job description and now I've got twice as much work to do."

"Have you seen Hover around?" asked Buzz.

"I think he's in a meeting with Greybee and the consultant," replied a bee named Polly. "I went past his office and the door was closed. They've been in there for over an hour."

"I wonder what they're talking about," said Stripes.

"Probably which employees they're going to lay off," replied Polly. "Imagine that - getting paid to go to a hive and tell the Queen who to lay off and then flying off with a nice fat fee for your services."

"Well, I hope they're done within five minutes," said Buzz. "I'm supposed to see Hover for my performance appraisal."

"Oh, please," said Polly as she rolled her eyes, "what a joke! I had mine this morning. I went in and my manager had a spreadsheet of things called 'KPIs' - things like the number of flights I took, the weight of my nectar delivered, foreign matter in the nectar and number of days missed due to bad weather. Then I was given my score. I thought, okay, I got a *score*. So what? What does that mean? It's a number. Meanwhile, this hive is going down the drain and bees like Hover and Greybee are worried about performance appraisals!"

A few minutes later Hover called Buzz to tell him that he was ready to see him. Buzz went to Hover's office and closed the door.

"Thanks for coming in, Buzz," said Hover. "Have a seat. Let's see, where did I put your folder? Oh yes, here it is. Okay. I'll give you a copy of your appraisal so that we can look at it together." He handed Buzz several sheets of paper stapled together. "Now then - the first section of the appraisal relates to your targets for the past year. I'm very happy to say that you met or exceeded all of them. Your numbers are very good. And by the way, I want to congratulate you on your performance during the big storm last autumn. You went above and beyond your regular duties. I want you to know that your effort was noticed and appreciated."

"Thanks very much," replied Buzz automatically. He had to think about what Hover was talking about. The big storm? Last autumn? It had been nearly a year ago! True, it had been a challenging day, but Buzz had practically forgotten about it. He didn't remember Hover saying anything to him at the time. Buzz had assumed that management weren't impressed by his efforts. It was nice to know - months later - that his work hadn't gone unnoticed. But that's how it went around the Luna hive - everything was done by the book, including employee reviews.

After around 20 minutes of running through yet more measures that Buzz felt he had no control over, Hover finally moved on. "Very well then, let's move on to your leadership capabilities. It says here... "

Unable to hold back his frustration any longer, Buzz cut across Hover without thinking. "Excuse me, but may I ask a question?" he asked.

Initially shocked, Hover put down the papers. "Okay. I suppose that's why we're here. For a 'healthy exchange of ideas.'"

"Well, just between you and me, aren't you concerned about the problem at Farmer John's wildflower meadow?" asked Buzz.

"Of course I am," replied Hover. "And I believe that the appropriate steps are being taken."

"With all due respect," said Buzz, "you may think so, but among the bees there's great concern. They're confused. They don't know what the solution is. They're starting to talk. They're looking for something positive."

"I understand," said Hover thoughtfully. "I'll discuss this with Greybee. Perhaps an email from the Queen herself would be in order. Something that every bee could read."

"You mean some sort of formal announcement?" asked Buzz.

"Yes. Something reassuring from the very top." With eyes closed, Hover smiled with satisfaction at this idea. He then directed his gaze at Buzz. "Are *you* confident in what our Queen has instructed?"

"It's not for me to say," replied Buzz, "but it seems to me that the main problem - the loss of the wildflower meadow - is not being addressed. I'd be willing to look into some different solutions… things that might involve taking some calculated risks and looking for new sources of nectar."

Hover looked uncomfortably at the floor for what seemed like an age. He was torn between his obligations to Greybee and his personal feelings. Looking up at Buzz he broke the silence with a decisive "Fair enough". He leaned towards Buzz. "I'll tell you what I'll do. I like you, Buzz. I'm going to give you a chance to give us some ideas. I can only give you one day to get your thoughts organised. I'll see you back here tomorrow at the same time. You're a smart and capable bee and I think you can make a contribution. I'm going to take a risk and see what you can come up with."

Appreciating his manager's sudden and dramatic change of style, Buzz thanked Hover for the opportunity and made a quick exit.

As he left Hover's office, Buzz felt apprehensive but he relished the challenge. He immediately headed for the hive library and logged on to the research portal. He was convinced that while the loss of the local wildflower field was a significant challenge to the very survival of the hive, the problem wasn't being addressed properly. The ideas offered by Wingit seemed to represent more of the same stale approach that was typified by the boring performance appraisal he had just endured.

In his search for ideas, Buzz checked out relevant training he could do to improve his ability to find a solution. There were several online programmes that seemed useful, but he was worried about the cost. As far as he knew, the Luna hive had no personal development programme for bees. If he wanted to do these courses, he'd have to pay for them himself. That would mean collecting a lot of nectar!

That night, he and Stripes talked about the problem.

"The way management is approaching this," said Stripes, "it will be weeks before they make any decisions. We could be out of reserves by then! I don't understand their thought processes. No one listens to the bees on the front lines. We need some decisive action."

Buzz thought for a moment. "I've been researching some ideas and have come to some conclusions," he said.

"What?"

"Since the problem is the destruction of Farmer John's wildflower field," he said, "then there are two obvious solutions: Find another field or move the hive."

"Do you think that Queen Luna would ever move the hive?" asked Stripes.

"I don't know," shrugged Buzz. "But it seems to me that every idea needs to be on the table. We can't afford to limit our thinking. Old ideas aren't going to work."

Stripes thought for a moment. "I've heard of another field."

"Really?" said Buzz. "Where?"

"It's very far away. It's called Smith's field, I think. You fly east through the woods and over the stream. I remember hearing about it from some of the older bees. They said that when Farmer John allowed his big field to go to seed and get taken over by wildflowers, everyone stopped going to Smith's field because going to Farmer John's field was easier and you could get all the nectar you could carry."

"I suppose you could say that we got spoiled by having such an easy flight to a place that had everything we needed," said Buzz. He looked at Stripes. "I've made up my mind. Tomorrow, I'm going to Smith's field."

CHAPTER 4

"A CHANCE ENCOUNTER"

The next day dawned bright and clear - a fine day for flying.

The new flight plans were not yet available from Leadbottom, who was still labouring in his office with his charts and rulers. Consequently, most of the bees who would ordinarily be taking flight to collect nectar from Farmer John's wildflower field were instead milling around in the common areas of the hive, unsure of what to do.

"Be patient," said Hover to his team, apparently back to his usual officious self. "As soon as management formulates a plan, I'm sure we'll be back in action."

"Are you going to Smith's field?" whispered Stripes to Buzz.

"Yes," he replied. "As soon as Hover goes back to his office, I'm going to take off."

Sure enough, a few minutes later Hover went into his office and closed the door.

"Good luck!" called Stripes as Buzz took off.

With a last look at the familiar hive, Buzz turned to the east and flew into the rising sun. He passed over open fields and the occasional house and barn. By the time the sun had risen higher and the shadows were shorter, Buzz came to the dark woods. For a bee, flying through the woods is a scary experience because it is more difficult to spot predators like spiders in their webs and hungry sparrows. Buzz pressed onward and after dodging some tall trees and steering clear of particularly shadowy areas he finally emerged from the woods. Before him he saw the silvery glint of the stream. With high hopes he followed the stream as it meandered through the rolling countryside.

Then, just before the sun reached its highest point in the sky, in the distance he saw a beautiful field of flowers in bloom.

The old stories were true!

Having reached the field, Buzz went from flower to flower, sampling the nectar of each. To his amazement he found strange new varieties of blooms that he had never seen before.

Could this be a problem? Would the honey makers at Luna hive be unable to process these new varieties?

Or would having new materials bring new opportunities?

Buzz didn't have the answer. He focused on the job at hand: collecting nectar.

Suddenly among the other bees working the field Buzz saw a familiar face. At the same moment, the other bee spotted Buzz.

"Hey friend, long time no see!" called Zippy from the next flower. "How have you been?"

"Pretty good, thanks," replied Buzz.

Buzz knew Zippy from seeing him at Farmer John's field. It was interesting to Buzz that Zippy was already working at Smith's field. *It didn't take him long to change fields*, thought Buzz. He wondered how many other bees from the Sola hive were also at Smith's field.

The hive ruled by Queen Sola was known to be rather "wild," at least within the highly organised confines of the Luna hive. The Sola hive was regarded as a freewheeling place where the Queen even mingled with the everyday bees, which never happened at Luna hive.

Buzz flew over to chat.

"How long have you been coming here?" asked Buzz.

"I've been coming here on occasion for several months," replied Zippy.

"But didn't I always see you at Farmer John's field?"

"Oh, sure," replied Zippy. "That's where I would usually go. But once in a while I'd come here, just to get some of this amazing nectar and to make sure I had a backup field."

"A backup field?"

"Yes. At Sola, every bee has at least two fields: a primary field and a secondary field. Some bees travel to three or four fields."

"Isn't that costly - in terms of your time?"

Zippy shrugged. "Well it paid off, didn't it? Farmer John's wildflower field is no more and there's no point crying about it. When something bad happens, we try to respond as quickly as we can. How about you, do you come here often?"

Buzz swallowed hard. He felt a bit embarrassed. He chose not to create a false impression, but to tell Zippy the truth.

"It's my first time here," he said as he inspected a sunflower. "At the Luna hive, we were unprepared for the closing of Farmer John's field. The bees are confused and morale is not very good. In fact, I'm not even supposed to be here today. None of the bees have received new flight plans. They're all back at the hive, just sitting around, waiting for instructions."

Zippy nodded thoughtfully. "So you decided to take a chance on a new field?"

"Yes," replied Buzz. "Don't get me wrong - the executives at Luna aren't bad bees. They're all very nice and have good intentions, but they're stuck in a routine. They've been doing the same thing for as long as anyone can remember. When we discovered that Farmer John's field was closed, the response was to call in a consultant and write a bunch of reports. Everyone's waiting to see what the Queen will decide. I'm not the type to just sit helplessly. I thought, why not take action? I had nothing to lose." He looked around the colourful field. "This place is amazing! It's a long flight, but there's no reason why we can't make it work. After all, our two hives are practically neighbours and it's a long flight for you too."

"Yes, it's quite a journey," said Zippy. "Obviously no one is happy that Farmer John ploughed up his flowers. But that's a part of life, isn't it? The world is full of risk. You can't avoid it."

"That's true. I don't think that risk is something that we handle very well at Luna hive."

"Why don't you come back with me to Sola?" said Zippy. "It's not far out of your way. You can meet some of our team and see how we do things. You might get some ideas that you can take back to Luna."

Buzz stopped and thought for a moment. "That sounds interesting, but are you sure they'll let me in? Won't I get stung because I'm from another hive? At the Luna hive, the security guards are very aggressive."

Zippy laughed. "Don't worry - I'll get you a visitor pass. Come on, it will be fun. You can bring your load of nectar and we'll hold it for you until you return to your hive."

"I need to get back to the Luna hive before dark," said Buzz. "You know that we honeybees don't fly at night."

"No problem," replied Zippy. "If we leave now we'll have plenty of time."

Buzz had never visited another hive before and the idea was exhilarating and intriguing. He agreed and without delay they took off.

CHAPTER 5

"THE SOLA HIVE"

The flight to the Sola hive retraced the same route that Buzz had taken earlier. They followed the stream, passed safely through the dark woods and flew over houses and barns. Just as the Luna hive could be seen as a speck in the distance, Zippy veered to the south and within a few seconds the Sola hive came into view.

Zippy landed first while Buzz hovered nearby, safely out of range of the security guards. After a few minutes Zippy returned with a guest pass.

"Wow, that was fast," said Buzz as Zippy handed the entrance card to him. "At the Luna hive, if I want to apply for a guest pass, I need to submit an application in triplicate to the director of security. It can take several days for him to process it."

"Here at Sola, every bee is allowed two guest passes a month," shrugged Zippy. "It only takes a few minutes to get them from the front desk."

With Zippy leading the way, they made their way to the front entrance of the hive. After being checked in by the friendly security bee, they entered the big central atrium.

Instantly Buzz sensed a new and exciting type of culture. Here, bees of various ranks intermingled freely. He saw groups of bees having quick stand-up meetings, out in the open, where anybody could see them. At the Luna hive, meetings were always formal affairs. If you wanted to have a meeting involving more than one department you had to reserve the conference room. Sometimes the room was booked up all day, so you had to schedule your meeting well in advance.

The atmosphere inside the Sola hive was at first a bit disorienting for Buzz; it wasn't immediately clear where individual bees fitted in the hierarchy of the hive. Buzz was accustomed to a high degree of vertical organisation, where information flowed up to the Queen and her orders flowed back down. Here, it seemed as though ideas were flying around like - well, like bees flying around a meadow.

"What's going on over there?" asked Buzz, indicating one of the groups of bees who were standing around having an animated discussion.

"Oh, that's the product development team talking to some of the sales bees," said Zippy. "They have those little meetings all the time."

"What do they talk about?" asked Buzz.

Zippy laughed. "You're kidding, right?" Then he realised that Buzz wasn't kidding - Buzz really didn't know. "Here at Sola, the product development bees want to hear what our customers say," said Zippy. "The sales bees are in contact with our customers every day. They're a good source of customer feedback."

"So you develop products based on what customers say?"

"Yes, why not?" replied Zippy. "Last month we brought out a new line of orange blossom honey. It's something that our customers kept asking about. We scouted around and found a terrific source of orange blossom nectar. Top-grade stuff."

Buzz knew that it would be rude to ask where Sola had found orange blossoms - but he made a mental note to investigate where the source might be.

"Hey Buzz, are you hungry?" asked Zippy. "I'm starving. How about a bite to eat?"

"Sounds good," said Buzz. "Lead the way!"

Buzz followed Zippy down a busy corridor. They passed a door with a sign over it that said "The Idea Factory."

Buzz stopped and turned to Zippy. "What's the Idea Factory?"

"It's just what it sounds like - the place where new ideas are offered and discussed," said Zippy. He peered into the room. On the wall was a big whiteboard with ideas written on it. "I think we'd better move along," he said to Buzz. "We can't have you flying away with our trade secrets!"

They came to the spacious lunchroom. On the walls Buzz noticed posters and signs with various phrases and slogans:

"Look for New Flower Fields!"

"There Is No Failure - Only Learning!"

"Your Beehaviour Is What Counts!"

"Some of these posters are a bit cheesy," admitted Zippy as they stood in line, "but they help convey a team attitude. Every bee knows that their individual contribution is important."

In a few minutes they were sitting with their trays at a table by a window.

"Tell me," said Buzz as he sipped his cup of nectar, "How did the Sola hive respond when Farmer John ploughed up his field?"

"It's been a challenge," replied Zippy. "Obviously the wildflower field was a very big source of nectar for us, as it was for you too. While we had other sources lined up - such as Smith's field - there was talk of cutting expenses by reducing bee numbers. To explore the possibilities, the Queen organised a series of open meetings where anyone could voice an idea."

"Really?" said Buzz. "Anyone?"

"Yes, anyone," replied Zippy. "More than one bee proposed that if we focused more on premium honey, we could actually sell less of it because we'd be able to charge more."

"Like orange blossom honey," said Buzz.

"Exactly," replied Zippy. "It's more difficult to make than regular wildflower honey, but people are willing to pay more for it. Though it's still early in the game, it looks like we'll be able to make up for the loss of Farmer John's field and not have to reduce our workforce. Laying off bees is sometimes a reality, but the Queen doesn't want to weaken the hive by reducing our numbers."

"You must have individual goals and KPIs," said Buzz, pleased he could remember the new management term he'd so recently learnt from Greybee.

"Yes, we do and we take them very seriously, but they're developed with everyone's input. Take Farmer John's field, it was a big source of wildflower nectar. Now it's gone and the only wildflowers left are several miles away. Clearly, we needed to adjust our KPIs to reflect this new reality. This was done with input from several departments."

"Not just from the Queen," remarked Buzz.

"She has her say," smiled Zippy, "but she usually lets the department managers make the decisions with their teams. She's more like a coach than a boss."

"Does everyone have a job description?" asked Buzz.

"Yes, but we do a lot of cross-functional working. We believe that it's important for every bee to be familiar with every role. It helps you to see the big picture."

Buzz took a sip of his nectar. "The Luna hive tends to be compartmentalised. Managers have meetings with their staff in which they just hand out instructions. You'd never think of offering an idea to someone in another department - they'd be deeply offended, like you were disrespecting them. When we learned that Farmer John had ploughed up his wildflower field, the Queen hired an outside consultant. The guy came into the hive and made all sorts of recommendations about creating new functions and developing new KPIs. Maybe I'm weird, but the things he said didn't seem to address the problem."

"We do things a bit differently around here," said Zippy. "We get rid of processes that don't produce the value that our customers want. We like to see ourselves as a 'learning hive,' and we continually make improvements to our operation. Take this nectar, for example, it's a special blend from a variety of flowers. It's the first step towards a new premium honey. It was developed after a bee made a suggestion based on what a customer had said to her. I guess you could say that we're always open to innovation and change. Everyone knows that if they have an idea, the other bees will listen to it."

"You must hire only highly qualified bees," remarked Buzz. "Real geniuses."

"Not really," smiled Zippy. "In fact, our Queen believes that a bee's ability to engage with the other members of the team is more important than their technical skills. You can teach almost anyone to collect nectar or build a honeycomb, but it's more difficult to change someone's behaviours. You've probably heard the expression, 'hire slow, fire fast.' That's what we try to do. We try to make sure a new bee is a good fit in our culture before we sign them up. But if someone just can't understand how we do things, it's better for them and for us if we make a separation."

Buzz thought of the many manager bees at Luna hive who for years had been lurking behind the closed doors of their offices. They clung to their positions and guarded their turf, even if it meant the hive didn't innovate or stay ahead of the game.

He glanced at the clock on the wall. "This has been a wonderful visit, but I'd better be going. It will be sunset soon."

"Right," said Zippy. After placing their trays on the tray return counter, they headed back towards the main atrium. As they walked, Buzz was amazed to see so many bees interacting freely but without any of the chaos that he had expected to find in such an unstructured environment. There was order and logic to it all but it was hidden under the surface.

Zippy and Buzz turned a corner.

Suddenly Buzz saw a regal bee who radiated benevolent authority. Engaged in a conversation with a worker bee, she looked up and saw Zippy and Buzz.

Buzz froze, his knees began to shake and his mouth went dry.

"Hello Queen Sola," said Zippy.

Buzz didn't know what to do. It was the first time in his life he had been face to face with a queen.

"Hello Zippy," replied the Queen.

"Queen Sola, please allow me to introduce Buzz," said Zippy. "He's visiting from Queen Luna's hive."

"Ah, Queen Luna," said Queen Sola with a smile. "I haven't

seen her in quite a while. I suppose both of us are too busy with our hives to go out very much. Please give her my regards when you see her."

"Umm, of course," replied Buzz. He felt awkward because he had never spoken to Queen Luna and was in no position to convey anyone's greetings to her. So he just smiled and tried not to look nervous.

"Anyway, nice to meet you, Buzz," said the Queen. She then turned to talk to another bee. Zippy and Buzz continued on their way.

"Wow," said Buzz. "For a queen, she's friendly."

"What are queens supposed to be like?" replied Zippy.

"Come to think of it, I don't know," said Buzz as they approached the big atrium and the reception desk. "All I know about our Queen is that she's the one who has all the answers."

"I suppose it's different around here," said Zippy. "Our Queen expects *us* to come up with the answers!"

As the sun neared the western horizon, Buzz prepared for take off. Then he turned to Zippy. "Do you think it would be okay if I returned sometime, maybe with another bee or two? Just to have another chat?"

"It would be a pleasure," said Zippy. "Meanwhile, I suppose I'll be seeing you at Smith's field?"

"Well, I assume so," replied Buzz. He hadn't yet received his new flight instructions, but to what other field could he go? It seemed absurd that a decision hadn't yet been made. "Yes," he said with more confidence. "I'll see you over at Smith's field."

With those words he waved goodbye and took off.

CHAPTER 6

"BRINGING THE OUTSIDE IN"

It was not too long before Buzz arrived back at the Luna hive. It felt good to be home!

He went first to the nectar delivery room and unloaded his nectar.

"Where did you get this nectar?" asked Zag, the bee in charge of the supply chain. "Has it been authorised?"

"Not exactly," said Buzz. "I know it's an unfamiliar type, but there's plenty more where it came from. Just put it somewhere and we'll sort it out later."

With a heavy sigh and a shake of his head, Zag accepted the delivery.

On the way to the bee lounge, Buzz ran into Stripes.

"How was your trip to Smith's field?" she asked breathlessly.

"Terrific," he replied. "It's far away, but we can definitely get there and return safely in a day. But something even more exciting happened - I saw an old friend there named Zippy. He invited me back to his hive for a visit so we went there on the way home. He showed me around the hive and we talked about how they run their business."

"Doesn't Zippy live at Sola hive?" asked Stripes. "They're known to be a wild bunch - not disciplined like us."

"But they *are* disciplined - only in a different way," said Buzz. "In fact, I'd say they're incredibly disciplined. The closing of Farmer John's wildflower field hasn't got them worried. They've got a plan. Do you want to know something? Zippy has already been to Smith's field and more than once. He's been there many times. At Sola, every bee has a backup field. It makes sense, doesn't it? Why put all of your eggs in one basket?"

"It sounds very sensible," said Stripes. "I wish we could plan ahead like that and be ready to respond when conditions change."

Hover spotted Buzz and came over to him. "Where have you been all day?" he asked.

Buzz swallowed hard. "I'll be honest with you. I went to a place called Smith's field to see if it was suitable for nectaring. While I was there I ran into Zippy, who took me to Sola hive for a visit. I just got back a few minutes ago."

Hover looked at Buzz as though he were crazy.

"You're going to fire me, aren't you?" asked Buzz. "Look, I'm sorry, but you did give me one day to come up with an idea about how we could make a difference, and, and..."

"No, I'm not going to fire you," Hover interrupted. "At least not until I've heard the entire story."

Buzz eagerly told Hover about all that he had experienced at Sola hive.

"At Sola hive," Buzz said, "it's all about the culture. They combine logic and emotion – they make lots of great honey but their bees are happy and engaged too. Around here - you'll forgive me for saying this - we only think about what's *supposed* to work instead of what *really* works. We've got our noses buried so deep in the operations manual that we don't see how the world is changing all around us. When Farmer John ploughed up his field, we were caught flat-footed. We were unprepared."

"Are you saying that Sola has a complete plan in place?" asked Hover. "Really?"

"No, not a complete plan," said Buzz. "They were surprised too. But they take sudden changes in their stride. They *expect* change, even if they're not sure what that change is going to be. The culture of the hive is designed to be flexible and respond to what the world throws at them."

If Hover had a chin, he would have rubbed it. Instead he looked thoughtful. "I heard that you brought back some new varieties of nectar. Were they from this '*Smith's field*' place?" he said.

"Yes," replied Buzz. "Sola hive is using them to develop new lines of honey. I thought that our production guys could have a look at them. With our major source of wildflowers gone we're going to have to adjust our product line and I thought there was no point in waiting."

"True," replied Hover. "There's no point in waiting. In fact, Greybee is still in her office. We're going to see her right now."

"Right now?" said Buzz. "Why?"

"So that you can tell her yourself what you saw at Sola hive," replied Hover. "I want to get this information to the Queen."

"Are you serious?" said Buzz as Hover led him and Stripes along the corridor to the executive wing of the hive.

Hover stopped and turned to him. "Just between us, I'm worried. What I see around here is what I've heard is called '*paradigm paralysis.*' "

"I've heard of that," said Stripes. "It's the inability or refusal to see beyond current ways of thinking. It's what my old grandpa called 'being stuck in the mud.'"

Hover nodded. "Wingit has recommended a load of changes but I don't see them making any difference. The fundamental structure of the hive is the same as it's always been. We've got nothing to lose by taking a chance. That's how I see it."

Greybee was available. She agreed to meet with them and she listened to the story that Buzz told about his trip to Smith's field and the Sola hive.

"Hover, what do you think of our situation?" she asked. "Are the changes that Wingit proposed finding acceptance with the bees on the front lines?"

"To be honest Greybee, we're having a difficult time," replied Hover. He pulled out his notebook. "I'd like to share with you some of the comments I've received in the past few days."

"Comments?" said Greybee. "From the bees?"

"Yes - I asked them for their feedback," said Hover.

"That's highly unusual," said Greybee, "but please continue."

"Here's a sample," said Hover.

"Why all this change?"

"Why can't we go back to the way things were?"

"The managers don't care about us; they just want us to work harder and produce more."

"Even though market conditions have changed, everything remains the same."

"We're in the dark. What's going on?"

"The new processes have increased our workload but our products are no better."

"The hive says to do it this way today and then tomorrow it's different. There's no consistency."

"We have ideas about how to make our products better but no one ever listens."

When Hover had finished, Greybee sat in silence.

"Don't the bees get the memos we send?" she eventually said.

"At the Sola hive, managers don't send memos," said Buzz. "They talk."

"That seems old-fashioned," said Greybee. "I thought that sending email blasts was the modern way of communicating."

Just then the door opened. It was Queen Luna. She peered into the room.

Buzz held his breath. He tried not to look directly at her Royal Highness.

"I'm sorry Greybee, I didn't realise you were in a meeting," said the Queen.

Greybee stood up to move towards the door. "Really, it's no problem - what can I do for you?"

Queen Luna handed Greybee a sheet of paper. "This is the memo regarding the new flight assignments. We had hoped to have them tonight but they will be delayed until tomorrow. Please send an email blast to the hive. Thank you."

Greybee glanced at Hover, then back to the Queen. "May I tell the bees the reason for the delay?" she asked.

The Queen waved her antennae. "It's something to do with Leadbottom's charts. But the reason is not important. Do the bees really care? After all, they'll have another half-day off from flying! Why should they question it?"

"Queen Luna, excuse me," said Buzz. Everyone looked at him in astonishment. He had spoken directly to the Queen!

"Yes, what is it?" she asked.

"If you want me to, I can lead a group to a place called Smith's field tomorrow," said Buzz. "I was there today."

"Thank you for your suggestion," replied the Queen. "However, I think it's best if we stick to our plan. When the flight plans are approved, your Smith's field may very well be on the agenda."

With those words she left the room.

"I think that Queen Luna made herself very clear on this issue," said Greybee.

The door opened again. A bee entered and handed Greybee

another sheet of paper. "These are the sales projections for the next six months," said the bee.

Greybee studied the document. Her face was serious. "It says here," she began, "that with the closing of Farmer John's field and without new sources of nectar and new product development, we can expect sales to decline by fifty percent." She put the paper on her desk. "It will be a disaster. I think we need to start to prepare for layoffs."

Hover stepped forward. "Greybee, I think that what Buzz saw at the Sola hive could be very useful. I understand that the Queen has made a commitment to the programme that Wingit has devised. But we're in trouble. No one wants layoffs. Having heard what Buzz has said, I sincerely believe that we can make a big difference to our hive - to our future - if we try to change the culture here and take some risks."

"You really think that those wild bohemians at Sola hive can teach us something?" said Greybee.

"They're not as wild as they appear," said Buzz.

"Yes, I think they can teach us something," said Hover. "Here's what I propose. Make my team a pilot programme. I've got fifty bees in my department. I say, turn us loose. I'll send a small group of three or four bees back to Sola hive to learn more. The rest of us will brainstorm. Nothing will be off limits. Any idea will be considered. We'll go to Smith's field and any other field we can get to. We'll bring back what we find. We'll work with the product development guys to create products that use the resources that we have and we'll work with the sales bees to make sure we deliver what our customers want."

Greybee thought for a moment. Then she spoke.

"I suppose we have nothing to lose by trying. But we need to keep it off the Queen's radar, at least until we get some results. Wingit's plan has a small provision for research and development. That's what we'll call it - 'R & D'. Go ahead with your proposal, but keep it quiet. I don't want to start a major discussion about this with the Queen and Wingit. They might order us to stop it. Okay?"

"Agreed," said Hover. He turned to Buzz and Stripes. "Ready for a challenge? Good! Let's get started!"

CHAPTER 7

"TIME TO COME CLEAN"

Without delay Hover called a meeting of his team in the hive's big conference room, which was fortunately available at short notice.

"Folks," said Hover to the fifty bees assembled around the podium, "The Luna hive is facing a tremendous challenge. As some of you may have heard, Farmer John ploughed his wildflower field into the earth. Every blossom there is gone."

The room was silent.

"Is that why flights were suspended?" asked a bee.

"Yes," replied Hover.

"Why didn't the Queen tell us?" queried another.

"I ask you not to worry about that right now," replied Hover, "from this moment onwards, we're looking forwards, not backwards. This team has been chosen by Greybee herself to play by a new set of rules. We're going to develop a new way of conducting ourselves. The path has been revealed to us by our friends at Sola hive."

A murmur went through the crowd.

"Isn't Sola a place where the bees just do what they want all day?" asked a third bee. "Where it's all fun and games?"

"I'll answer that," replied Buzz. "I visited Sola hive yesterday. I saw for myself how they operate. In a sense you're right, they *do* have fun. They have fun because they really love their work. They enjoy finding new species of flowers. They enjoy making the very best honey that they can. At Sola, every bee feels as though their job is important. From the bees who clean out the nurseries to the bees who serve next to the Queen herself, there is a sense that the hive is one big team. That's what this pilot programme is all about. It's about the hive *giving* you more and at the same time *expecting* more. Let me ask you guys a question - how many of you feel as though you're working at your highest potential? Raise your hands."

A few hands went up. Most of the bees just sat quietly.

"And how many of you are just coasting from day to day? It's okay to be honest. Tell me the truth."

Nearly every hand went up.

"We're going to change that," said Hover. "Buzz, why don't you start by telling the group what you learned at the Sola hive?"

A few minutes later, when Buzz had finished, a sense of excitement filled the room. Hands shot up in the air as curious bees shouted out their questions as Hover tried to bring some order to the meeting.

"How does Sola hive decide what fields to fly to?"

"Do they really ask their customers to give them product feedback?"

"Does the Queen really walk among the ordinary bees?"

"Do they really have a place called the Idea Factory where any bee can offer suggestions?"

Buzz tried to answer each question as best he could. The bees wanted to know everything.

"Okay, let's take a break from the questions," Hover said eventually. "As part of this pilot project, the Sola hive has graciously invited a small group of our bees to visit them and learn more about how they operate. This education team will consist of four bees. Buzz and Stripes will be two of them but I need two more volunteers."

Every hand in the room shot up.

Hover chose two candidates - Digger, from the honey production department and Mason, who was a customer account administrator.

After a quick briefing the four bees took off for Sola hive.

Hover told his team to go about their usual business for the rest of the day.

Just before sunset the four bees returned from Sola hive. They hurried to the conference room as Hover assembled his team. Within a few minutes the meeting was convened.

After the four bees had presented a quick overview of the trip, Hover asked Buzz to step forward and deliver his notes.

"Don't you want to be the one to deliver them?" asked Buzz. "After all, you're the manager."

"You went there, so *you* tell them," said Hover. "Remember, we're no longer concerned about rank. We only care about results."

"Right," said Buzz. He then presented the group with four ideas that they might want to try:

1 Organise the collector bees into two groups: Scouts, who will look for new sources of nectar, and Collectors, who will harvest it.

2 Adopt a new set of values based on mutual cooperation and focus on the goal. For example: If you see bees who are overloaded, just go and help them. If you think that a plan isn't working, immediately tell your supervisor and work out how to change it. Listen to the ideas of other bees and give them the same respect as if they were your own ideas. Once an idea is agreed, commit to it one hundred percent. Take pride in your work, because every job done by every bee is important.

3 Communicate more. Share information freely. Don't wait for a formal staff meeting to share a concern - have a quick stand-up meeting anywhere, anytime.

4 Hover, the team leader, is your coach. It's his job to help you do the best work possible and to make sure you have the tools you need. If you trust Hover, he'll trust you.

Hover then opened the meeting to discussion. Whilst most of the bees were enthusiastic about the changes and understood the value of a positive hive culture, a few bees expressed doubt and fear. One or two flatly said that it wouldn't work.

"Make no mistake," said Hover in reply, "the stakes are very high. This hive faces a serious challenge. We believe we can overcome it and become even better than before. But to succeed, we need everyone to give one hundred percent. In the old days, we'd carry those bees who didn't pull their weight. We tolerated slackers. The hive was full of bees who would sit at their desks all day and shuffle papers. Those days are over. From this moment forward, we need every team member to contribute. I will work with you to help you. I'll give everyone a fair chance. For those bees who can't get on with the programme, I will have you transferred out."

Everyone - even the doubters - agreed that this was a very fair deal. The meeting broke up and with a renewed sense of purpose the bees began the process of reinventing their team.

CHAPTER 8

"A VISIT FROM QUEEN LUNA"

A week later, Hover went to see Greybee in her office.

"I've been hearing good things about *Team Hover*," said Greybee. "You've secured a new route to Smith's field, and I understand your collectors are bringing back new varieties of nectar that your product development bees think will make premium honey flavours. We can sell them at a higher price than regular honey."

"Yes and we've also scouted two other new fields," replied Hover. "They're very far away, but to help our collectors we're developing little backpacks that will allow them to carry food and water for longer flights."

"Very impressive," said Greybee. "In fact, I want to bring Queen Luna to visit the group today."

"Today?" replied Hover. "Do you think it's too early? We've only just begun. I'm sure the Queen has many other important things to attend to."

"Let me tell you something," said Greybee. "The Queen needs some good news and I thought that one of the important parts of your programme was transparency. No secrets. Am I right?"

Hover had no choice but to agree.

That afternoon, Queen Luna arrived at the section of the hive where Team Hover was based.

"I've never been here before," she said to the assembled bees. "You've made quite a nice work area." She picked up one of the tiny backpacks and inspected it. "What a brilliant idea! I'm sure our collector bees appreciate having food and water on their long flights."

The product development bee proudly stepped forward to present the Queen with a jar of a new variety of honey. Queen Luna tasted it. "Blueberry honey! I haven't had this in years! Where is it from?"

"A new field by the lake," replied Hover. "The scouts found it and we've started collecting from it. No other hive makes blueberry honey. It's an exclusive."

"I like that," replied the Queen. "My mother taught me long ago that you need to 'own your market'. I had forgotten what that meant. I suppose over the past few years we have become complacent."

At that moment the consultant, Wingit, pushed his way to the Queen's side.

"Queen Luna," he said, "I have very good news! Farmer John is allowing the wildflowers to return to his field. Apparently he's decided to let it stay fallow for another year. Within a few weeks, everything should be back to normal." He picked up one of the tiny backpacks. "You won't be needing these. Leadbottom will be handing out the customary flight plans. The hive can return to making the traditional wildflower honey that you've been making for years."

He handed the Queen a memo.

"Here," he said. "I've written the announcement for you. Just initial it and I'll send out the email blast. Then you can go back to your royal residence. You won't have to come down here again." Wingit looked around the room as if he were standing in a swamp.

The Queen looked at the memo. Then she looked around at Team Hover. She picked up one of the tiny backpacks. After looking at it, she put it back on the table.

"I'll give you my decision within the hour," she said. "Thank you, everyone. Please carry on as you were."

With those words she turned and left the room.

CHAPTER 9

"ANOTHER CHANCE ENCOUNTER"

Three weeks later, Buzz was flying over Farmer John's field. Sure enough, the wildflowers had been allowed to return and some of the young plants were forming blossoms.

At the edge of the field, Buzz spotted Zippy. He flew over to greet him.

"Hi, Zippy," cried Buzz.

"Hello, friend," said Zippy. "It's a beautiful day, isn't it? I wanted to tell you how much we enjoyed having you and your three colleagues over for a visit. I hope it was helpful."

"Yes, it was very helpful," replied Buzz.

"I haven't seen you since then," said Zippy. "How are things at Luna hive? Are you still doing things the same way you've always done them, or have you made the changes that we talked about?"

Buzz looked at Zippy. "I'll tell you exactly how things are," he said.

And then he told him…

CHAPTER 10

"A MYSTERIOUS CONCLUSION"

The question is....

What did Buzz say?

Did the Luna hive embrace the opportunity to change their culture to make them able to survive the uncertainties of the future? Or did they revert to their comfortable routines now that Farmer John's wildflowers had returned?

Like the bees in the Sola hive, we want to empower you to shape the destiny of the Luna hive. What would be your ideal conclusion to our tale or what do you think is the most likely outcome?

We invite you to write your own final "Chapter 10" for the book by visiting **www.thebeebook.com/chapter-10**. When asked, you will need to enter the code **TBB2016** so we know you are someone who has a copy of the book.

On the same page, you can also review the "Chapter 10s" written by other readers and rate each others' conclusions. We've set aside the following pages to record your ideas before you visit the website.

_____

_____

_____

_____

_____

_____

_____

_____

_____

"A MYSTERIOUS CONCLUSION"

"A MYSTERIOUS CONCLUSION"

_____

_____

_____

_____

_____

_____

_____

_____

_____

_____

_____

_____

_____

_____

_____

_____

"A MYSTERIOUS CONCLUSION"

_____

_____

_____

_____

_____

_____

_____

_____

_____

_____

_____

_____

_____

_____

_____

_____

THE BEE BOOK WEBSITE

At *www.thebeebook.com* you will find useful resources to use alongside The Bee Book to drive change in your organisation.

Here is a flavour of just a few of the resources we've included on the website:

- **"Chapter 10"** (*www.thebeebook.com/chapter-10*): As you saw at the end of the book, we've left the final chapter of the book for you to complete. By visiting this webpage you can:

  o Add your own final chapter to the book (remember to use code **TBB2016**)

  o Look at other readers' contributions and vote on your favourites

- **"Workshop"** (*www.thebeebook.com/workshop*): We have developed *The Bee Book Workshop* to support The Bee Book. This workshop is designed to embed the core principles covered in the story to successfully implement change in your organisation. With a range of delivery options including a Train the Trainer programme for independent and corporate trainers, there will be a workshop option to meet your needs. You can also purchase training materials and resources from this page on our website.

- **"Resources"** (*www.thebeebook.com/resources*): Here you will be able to access free tools to support you while using The Bee Book to drive change within your organisation. You will also be able to sign up to our mailing list and receive tips and ideas from Buzz and the team.

- **"Buzz's Blog"** (*www.thebeebook.com/buzzs-blog*): Follow Buzz's adventures and find out what new ideas Buzz has discovered about leadership, innovation, employee engagement and change.

SOCIAL MEDIA

You can also engage with us via social media:

Facebook: Like our page at
www.facebook.com/thebeebookdotcom

Twitter: Chat directly with Buzz at
www.twitter.com/thebeebook

You can contact us directly at:
info@thebeebook.com

SO WHY BEES?

Well, bees are workers (they visit 50 – 100 flowers during one collection trip), they work as a team, they resolve conflicts and adapt fast. Each bee knows and understands its position within the colony. They continually work to keep the hive alive. They plan ahead and constantly scan the environment within which they live to ascertain threats and opportunities alike.

Bees are agile creatures and constantly interact with one another. They have a well-defined social structure. This is necessary in any organisation if it is to be effective. We need bees to pollinate our crops and sustain our food supply. Bees are the only insects to produce food eaten by humans.

They are found on every continent (apart from Antarctica), have been around for millions of years. They have incredible endurance, flying up to six miles at a time.

Oh and they are quite likeable creatures too.

ABOUT THE AUTHORS

Craig Smith and Paul Rigby.

Having worked together since 2009 on various projects, Craig Smith and Paul Rigby decided it was time to write their own allegory and so The Bee Book was born.

Craig and Paul wrote The Bee Book to illustrate the importance of culture and how it affects the ability of organisations to change. Asked about the book, they said: "We love using stories to get people talking about change and what is important to them and their organisation. It's a skill we often neglect in our managers and leaders. If the book can get people talking and contrasting their own organisation with the Luna and Sola hives, that will be a great start."

Craig Smith supports some of the world's leading organisations who want to feel more connected, agile and to get their "mojo" back. He is passionate about employee engagement, visual communication tools and the power of conversation to drive change.

Craig is the owner of Flint Spark Consulting (*www.flintspark.co.uk*). He works with public and private sector clients to help them overcome the challenges they face when trying to change. Before founding Flint Spark in 2007, Craig worked for PepsiCo for six years in global operational and organisational development roles. Prior to that, Craig worked in operational roles within Royal Mail and Northumbrian Water.

Craig is a keen runner with thirteen international marathons under his belt and is a member of a select group of people who have run all of the six World Marathon Majors (Boston, Berlin, Chicago, Tokyo, London and New York). Craig has also trekked to the summit of the highest mountain in Africa, Mount Kilimanjaro in 2008.

Paul Rigby is a regular keynote presenter and facilitator at global industry conferences. Paul also consults with business partners and frequently assists them with their change, innovation, leadership and employee engagement efforts. Paul helps organisations to lead and successfully transform businesses in times of change. He has an incredible energy and passion plus an ability to translate his hands on experience to the business world. Paul has travelled to over 45 countries delivering keynote addresses and workshops to large multi-nationals, government organisations, SMEs, business schools and non-profit organisations.

Paul is an avid photographer (with a passion for wildlife) and a keen cyclist having completed five Pick 'n Pay / Cape Argus cycles races (a 108km route from Cape Town to Cape Point and back).

15463243R00077

Printed in Great Britain
by Amazon